Spell with Zip

Zip

Zip is a friendly space alien from planet Zee. He loves to learn. Zip uses his hands to speak to his friends. He can't wait to teach the people of planet Earth all about sign language. Zip is the captain of his spaceship.

Pella

Pella is Zip's best friend. She also comes from planet Zee. Pella is very brave. Although she is a little younger than Zip and Statz, she isn't afraid of anything and is always the first of the three friends to try new things.

Statz

Statz is in charge of computers on the spaceship. He loves gadgets. Statz uses his Zablet to help him and his friends out of sticky situations. He is excited to learn about planet Earth and all the people who live here.

Goober

Goober is an unexpected guest on the friends' adventures. A greedy and naughty space stowaway, Goober has the ability to change his colour and shape so is always jumping out and surprising Zip, Pella and Statz.

Zip's top tips

Zip and friends are here to help you talk in a fun new way - spell with your fingers and talk with your hands. Follow these top tips to get the most from their adventures:

- **Share the book together and enjoy the story**
- **Play with the signs**
- **Use Zip's alphabet to make your own words**
- **Visit Space School, enjoy the activities and have fun**
- **Watch out for Goober...**

SignSpell

Zip at the Theme Park

The spaceship has landed in a whole new world. Zip, Pella and Statz have never seen a place like this before. It doesn't look like planet Zee or planet Earth.

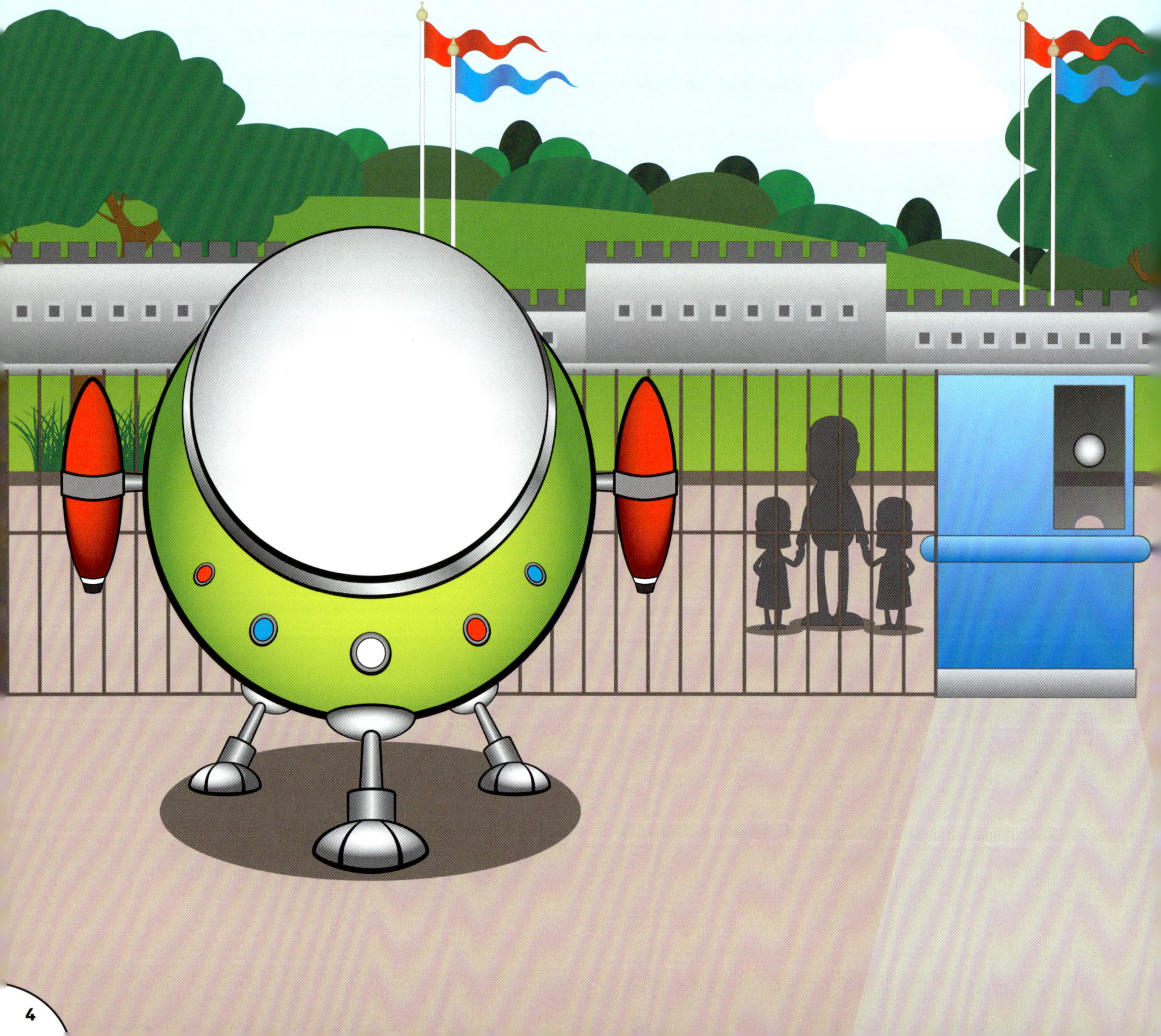

CRAZY KINGDOM
CRAZY KINGDOM
CRAZY KINGDOM

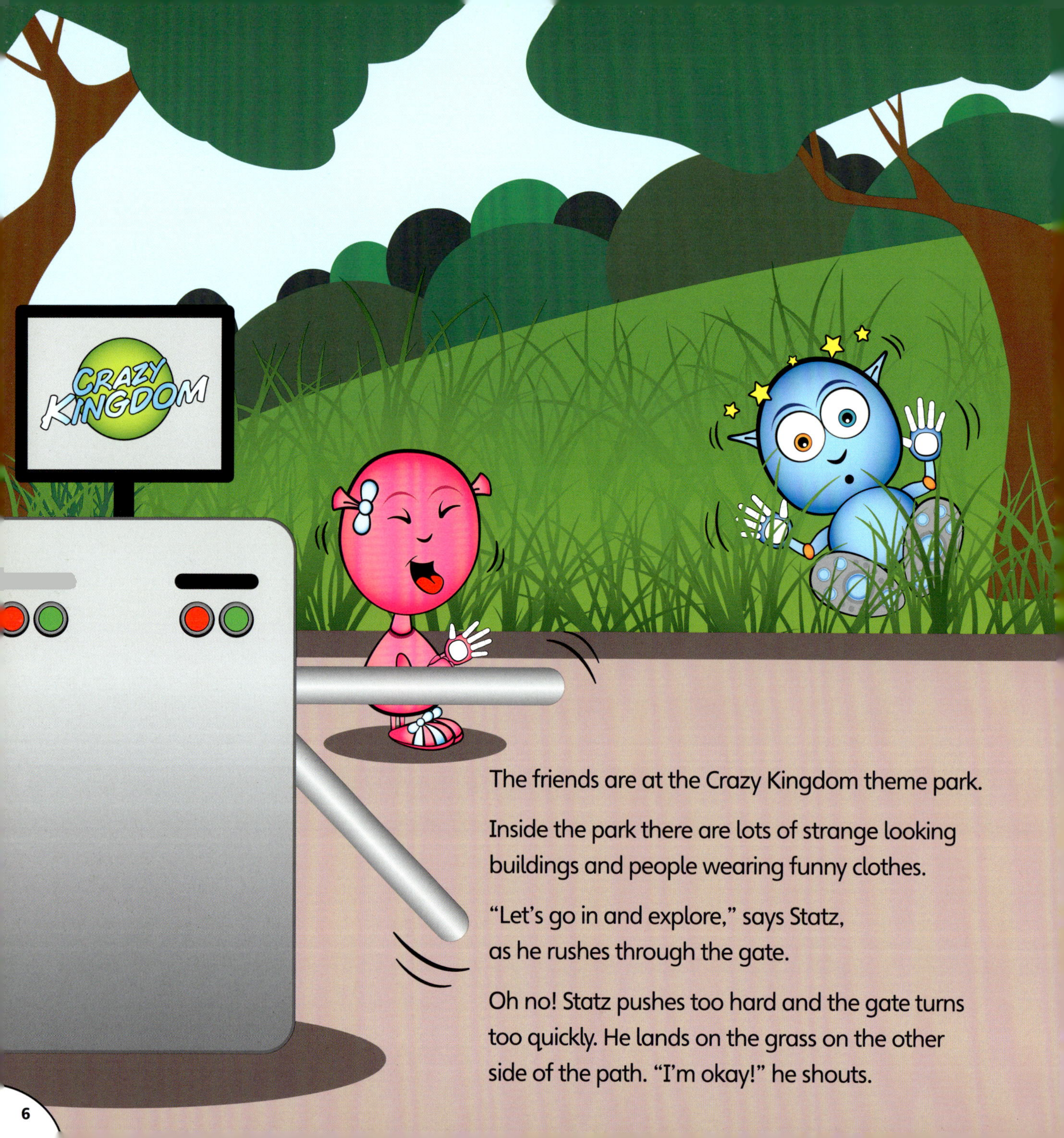

The friends are at the Crazy Kingdom theme park.

Inside the park there are lots of strange looking buildings and people wearing funny clothes.

"Let's go in and explore," says Statz, as he rushes through the gate.

Oh no! Statz pushes too hard and the gate turns too quickly. He lands on the grass on the other side of the path. "I'm okay!" he shouts.

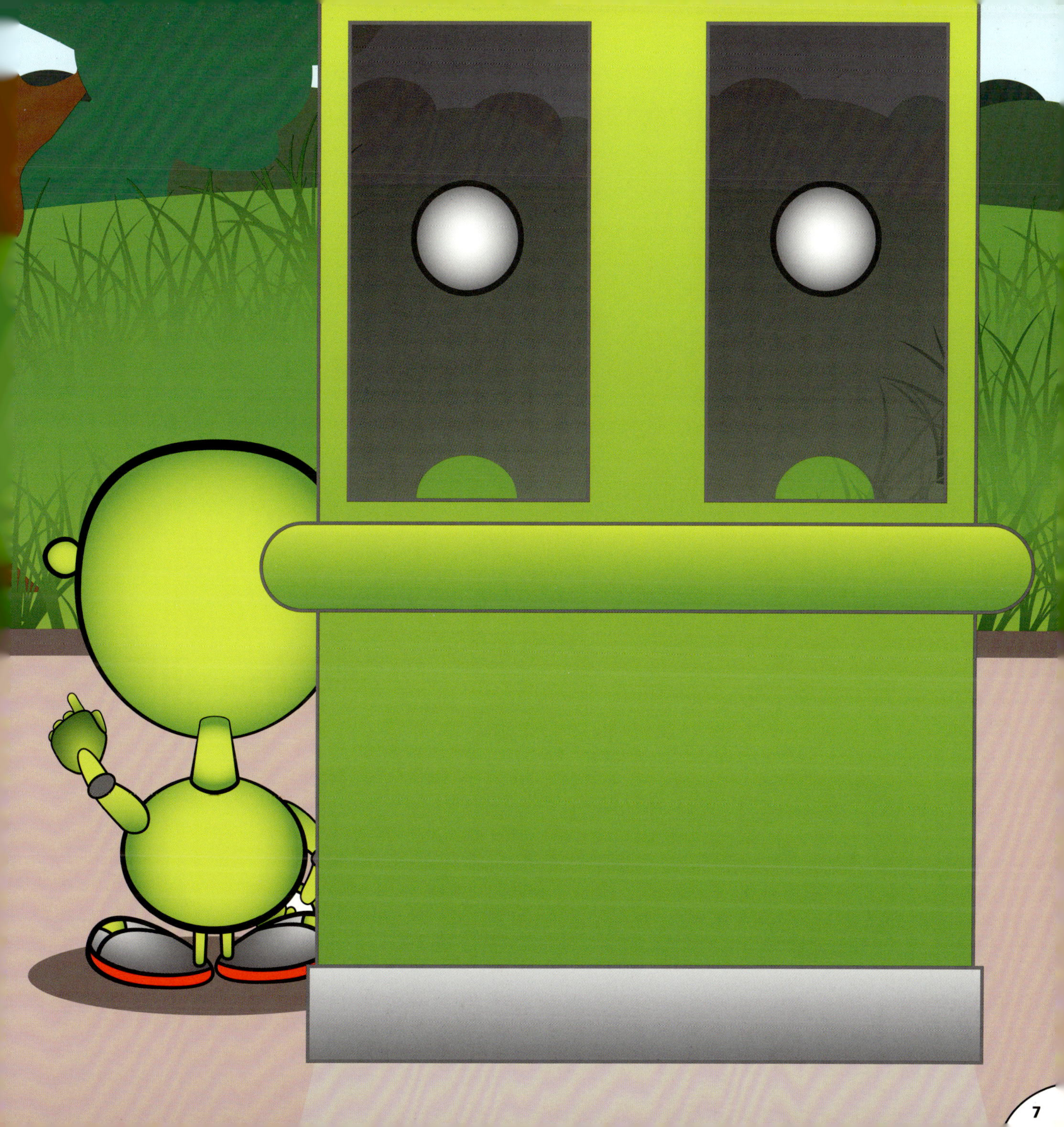

Inside the theme park there are juggling clowns with bright blue faces and clowns on stilts with bright purple faces. The clowns are walking around entertaining the humans.

There are lots of different rides to see. There are rides that spin, rides that loop-the-loop and rides that drop from a big height.

"I don't know which ride to go on first," says Statz.

Purple
x2

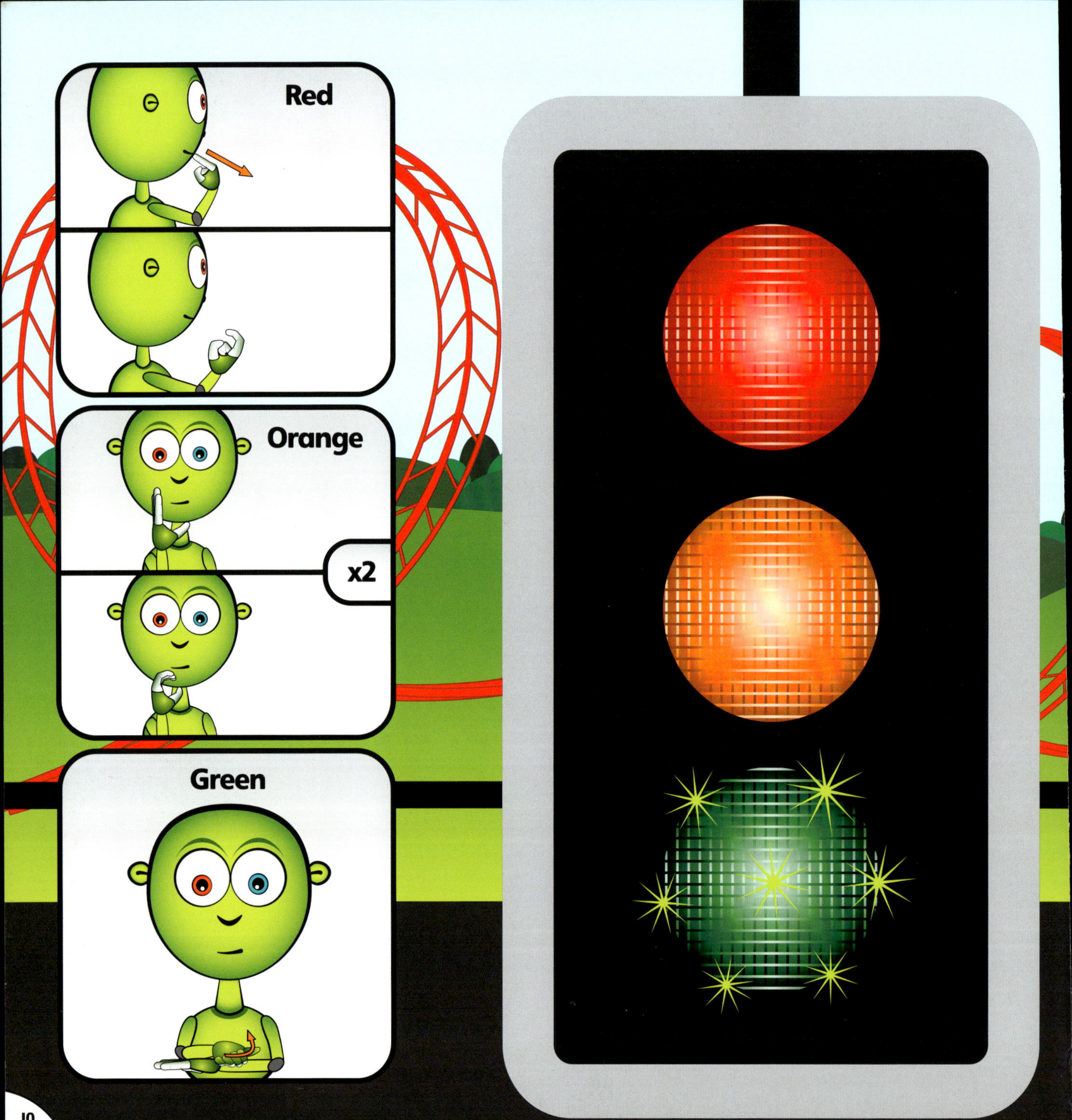
Red
Orange
x2
Green

“Let’s ride the biggest roller coaster first,” says Pella.

The friends wait for their turn and before long are locked safely in their seats.

The lights start to flash. Red. Orange. Green. Go!

The roller coaster is so fast that Zip, Pella and Statz are pushed back in their seats. They do five loop-the-loops and drop from up high. At the end of the ride they slam to a halt.

“That was amazing!” says Zip.

The next ride the friends go on is the Giant Teacups. Zip, Pella and Statz all climb into a big yellow teacup. They grab the wheel in the middle and start to spin.

Round and round and round they go. Faster and faster. As they spin they see a blur of colours: green, blue, purple, red, orange and yellow.

When the ride finishes the friends feel very dizzy.

"That was fun!" says Pella.

Yellow

Space School

Take a look at the map below and follow Zip's route through the theme park.
Can you spot some of the colours you have learnt so far?
See if you can spell each colour using Zip's alphabet.

When they stop feeling dizzy, the friends go to get something to eat. There are lots of different types of food to choose from.

Zip buys a jumbo hot dog with yellow mustard and red tomato sauce. Statz has a cone of chips covered in brown barbecue sauce. Pella buys a burger in a bun and fluffy pink candy floss for everyone to share later. “This food looks really tasty,” says Zip.

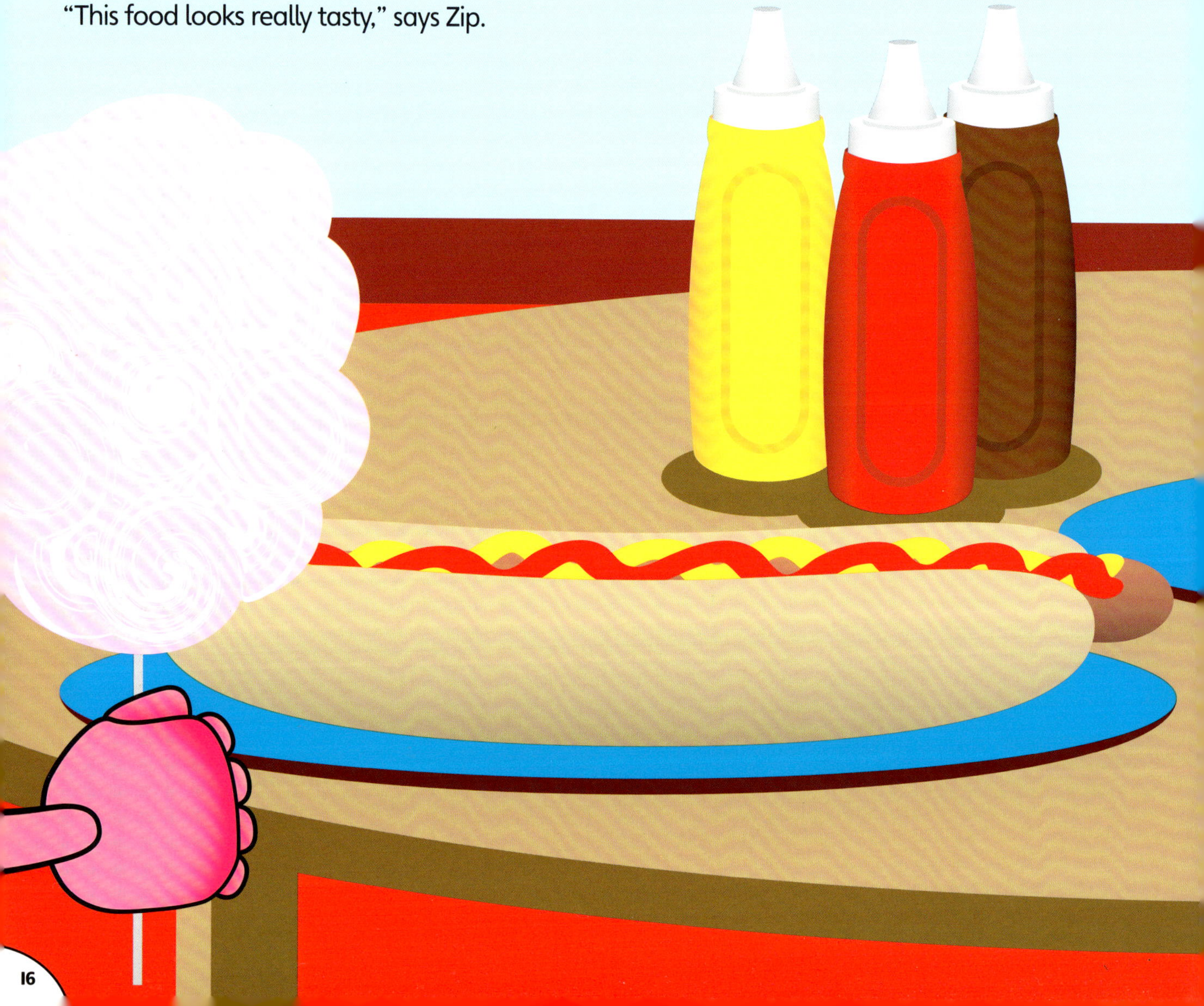

Brown

Pink

The friends have time for just one more ride. “Let’s go on the Water Ride,” says Pella.

They run to the ride and grab a yellow poncho each to stop them getting too wet. “I hope the water isn’t cold,” says Statz.

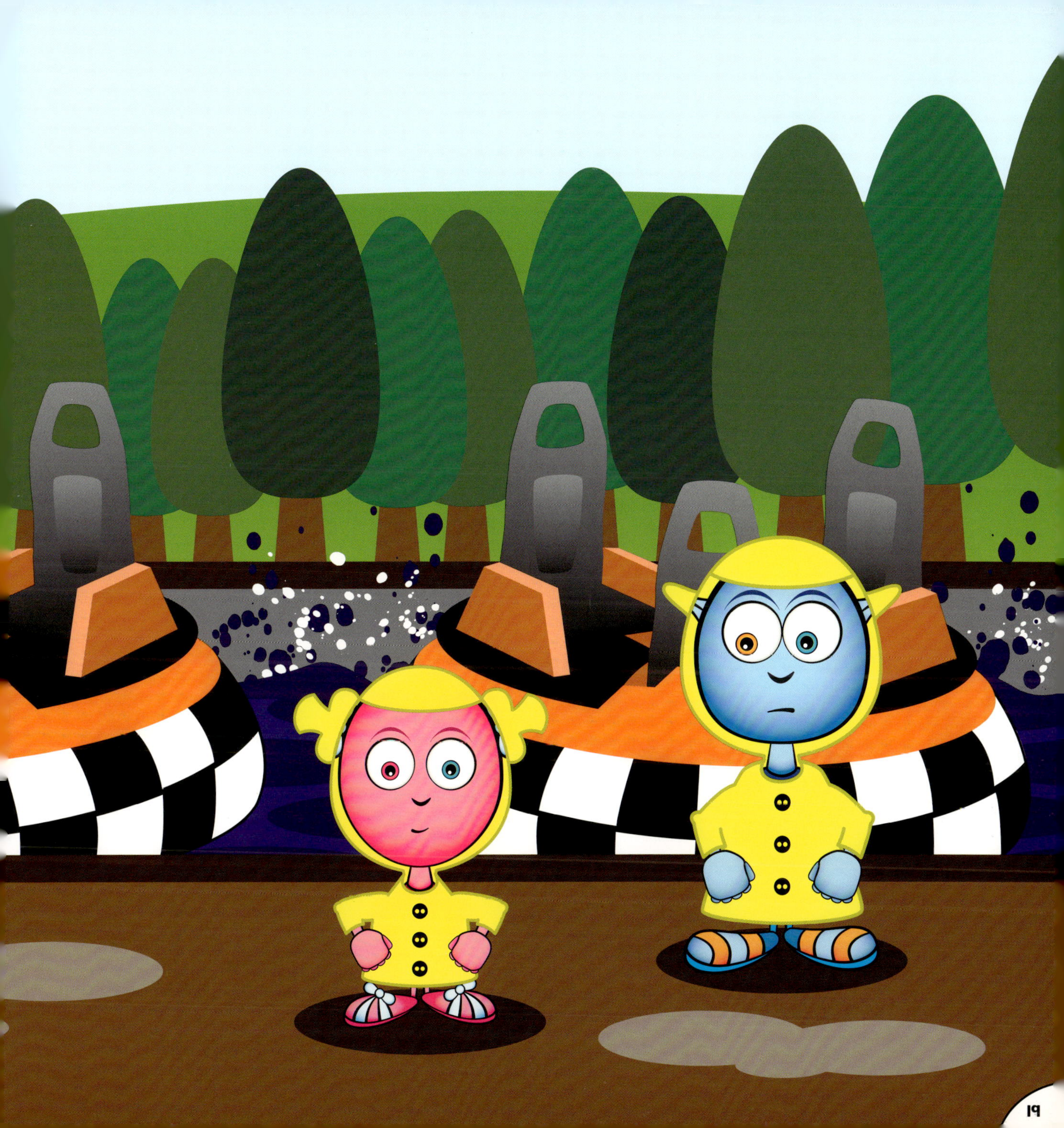

Zip, Pella and Statz jump into a black and white raft. The raft spins, turns and bumps along the rapids. They go through a dark tunnel before racing down a big water slide. “Hold on!” shouts Pella, “here comes the big splash.”

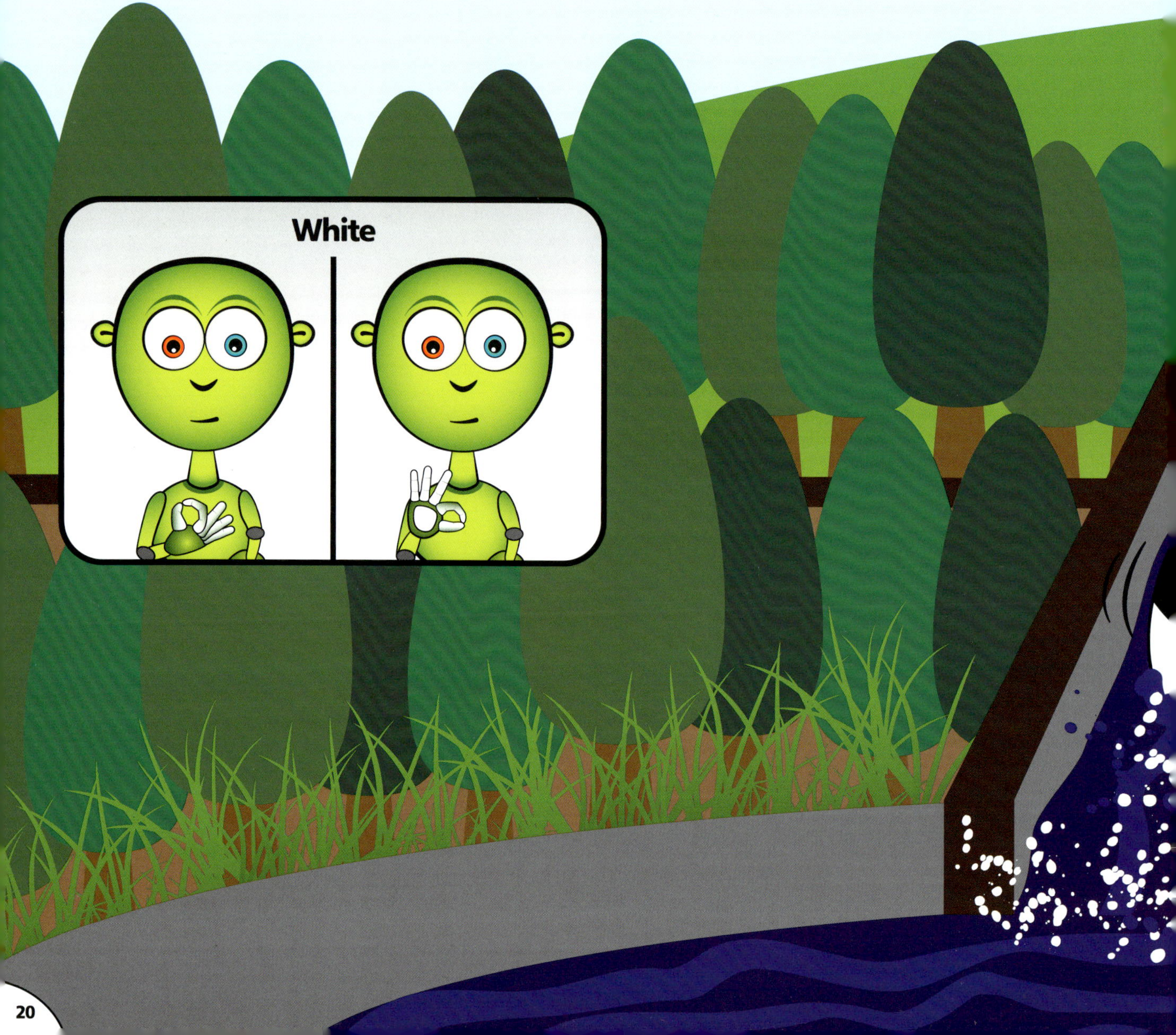

Black

The friends are soaked but they can't stop laughing. "That was so much fun," laughs Statz. "I wish we could do that again."

It's almost time to leave the theme park, but Zip wants to make one last stop.

Space School

Take a look at the pictures below.
Can you remember how to sign the colours?

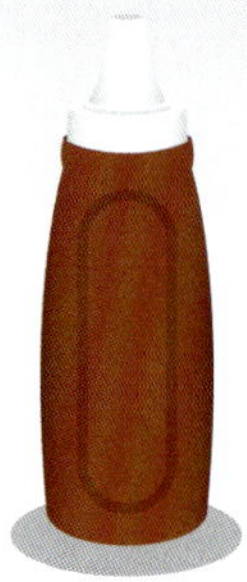

"I want to try to win a prize in the arcade," says Zip. Behind the glass he can see lots of different prizes.

"Get a box of green slime," says Pella.

"Go for the brown cowboy hat!" says Statz.

Zip is concentrating very hard. "I want to win a black and white football," he says. He presses the buttons and the claw drops down.

Zip, Pella and Statz all hold their breath. The claw comes back up holding a football, but this football isn't black and white.

GOOBER!

Zip's Signs

Green
Blue
Yellow
Brown
Red
Orange
x2
Purple
x2
Pink
White
Black

Fun things to do

Now that you have read all about Zip at the Theme Park,
here are some fun things for you to do:

- **Create your own ride - draw, describe or make**
- **How would you feel when the roller coaster light turns green?**
- **What would you eat and drink at a theme park?**
- **Do you think Zip liked his first ever jumbo hotdog?**
- **Where would Zip go on planet Zee for a fun day out?**
- **Teach a friend the signs for some colours around you**

First published 2013 by Signature

SignSpell® stories created by Signature
Designed and illustrated by Igloo Imaging Ltd.